W9-DAI-989

1 Mississippi, 2 Mississippi

A Mississippi Number Book

To: Donna Marks

Count Your Blessings, too!

Michael Shoulders

2 0 0 5

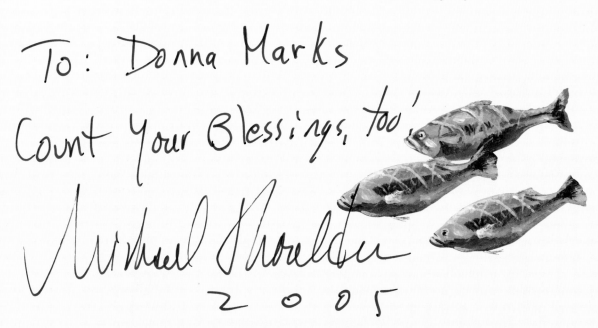

Written by Michael Shoulders and Illustrated by Rick Anderson

Special thanks to: Sundi Hurst with the City of Meridian's Parks and
Recreation Department, Meridian, Mississippi and Robert Pickenpaugh
of Pickenpaugh Pottery in Madison, Mississippi.

Sleeping Bear Press

310 North Main Street, Suite 300
Chelsea, MI 48118
www.sleepingbearpress.com

Printed and bound in Canada.

10 9 8 7 6 5 4 3 2 1

Library of Congress Cataloging-in-Publication Data

Shoulders, Michael.
1 Mississippi, 2 Mississippi : a Mississippi number book / written by Michael
Shoulders ; illustrated by Rick Anderson.
p. cm.
ISBN 1-58536-188-7
1. Mississippi—Juvenile literature. 2. Counting—Juvenile literature. I. Title:
One Mississippi, two Mississippi. II. Anderson, Rick, 1947- III. Title.
F341.3.S558 2004
976.2—dc22   2004024261

This book is appreciatively dedicated to Evelyn Vick, Chuck Maddox,
Debbie Nichols, and Margaret Pace. I am in awe of your talents
as educators and blessed to call each of you friend.

Special thanks to Dr. Pamela Harquail and Dr. Roger Wiemers.
You can't possibly understand the totality of how you lift the spirits
and souls of the students you serve. I wish you truly, truly knew!

For Amy—thanks for the vision.

MIKE

∾

Always for my wife, Merrie, whom I count on for support, who believes
in me, and is my best art critic, and who motivates me to create.
And I dedicate this book to my son, Denman, the actor and humanitarian.

Thanks also to everyone I used as models in my paintings. My hope
is that every reader appreciates the richness of the Magnolia State
from north Mississippi to the Delta to the Coast.

RICK

1 colossal waterwheel
spinning beneath a sky of blue.
Dunn's Falls is a great place to spend the day
to swim, fish, and barbeque.

In 1854 Irish immigrant John Dunn searched eastern Mississippi for the perfect location to build a cotton mill. He found his ideal spot 15 miles south of Meridian on a bluff towering above the Chunky River. By diverting a nearby stream Dunn formed a 65-foot waterfall that provided a continuous supply of waterpower. By 1860 Dunn completed a three-story mill with an adjoining waterwheel. The waterwheel harnessed the flowing water that turned the wheel which then turned a turbine to run the machinery.

During the Civil War Dunn's machinery was needed to manufacture war supplies such as blankets. After the war, Dunn's mill was used to make flour, hats, and even money. Eventually, Dunn's original mill and waterwheel deteriorated and were probably swept away by the Chunky River.

Today Dunn's Falls water park is open for fishing, picnicking, and camping. Even though Dunn's original mill and water- wheel are no longer there, an 1857 gristmill and waterwheel are on site.

one

1

2 magnolia blossoms
on one quarter make a pair.
Be sure to call out heads or tails
while it's turning in the air.

For many people, nothing represents Mississippi better than the fragrant magnolia blossom. In 1900 the children of Mississippi were asked to select a state flower. Although they picked the magnolia as their favorite, the legislature did not make it official until February 26, 1952. Two magnolia blossoms appear on the Mississippi quarter minted in 2002 as part of the 50 State Quarter® program.

The Mint's plan is to release a quarter for every state in the order that the state joined the Union. The Mississippi quarter reminds the world that Mississippi joined the United States in 1817 as the 20th state and is nicknamed "The Magnolia State."

The Latin phrase *"E Pluribus Unum"* translates to "Out of Many, One." This saying dates back to the founding fathers of America and represents America's goal to form one unified nation of many people from many varied backgrounds.

two

2

Since 1909 Highland Park in Meridian, Mississippi has been home to the famous Dentzel Carousel. The park was built near the end of the town's streetcar line and city officials wanted an attraction to draw crowds to the park on weekends. The town of Meridian bought a Dentzel carousel for $2,000. This carousel features 28 lifelike animals hand-carved from poplar or basswood and includes horses, deer, giraffes, goats, a lion and tiger. Dentzel Carousels are noted for their attention to detail right down to the veins in the horses' legs and their wind-blown mane. Today, Meridian's Dentzel Carousel is valued at over $1,000,000.

Gustav Dentzel (1840-1909) immigrated from Germany to the United States in 1860 and soon opened a cabinet shop. But Gustav returned to his family's tradition of building carousels when he established the G.A. Dentzel, Steam and Horsepower Caroussell Builder Shop.

In 1986 the Department of the Interior designated the Dentzel Carousel and Carousel House as National Landmarks.

three
3

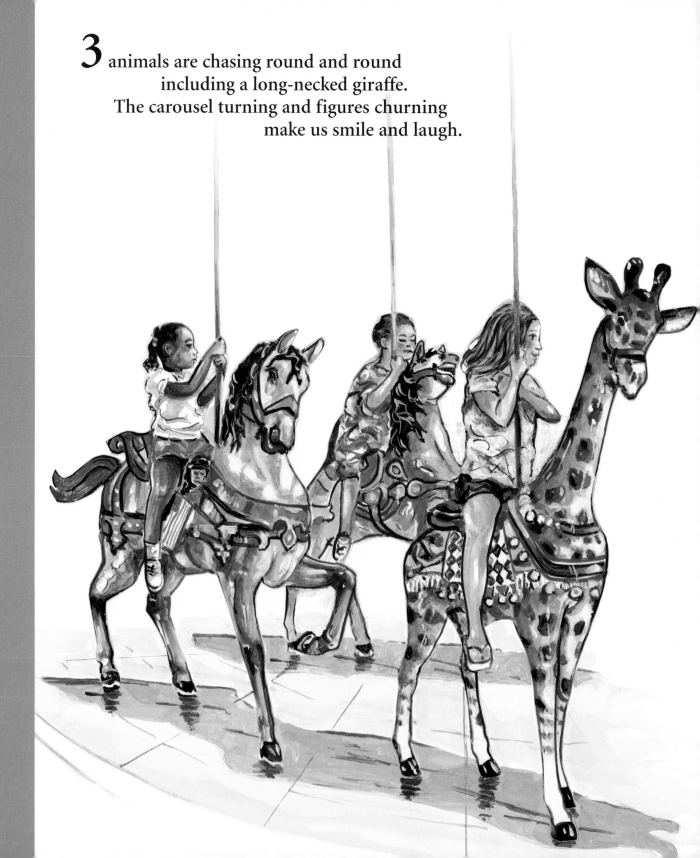

3 animals are chasing round and round
including a long-necked giraffe.
The carousel turning and figures churning
make us smile and laugh.

Mississippi is located in the Northern and Western Hemispheres, between 88 and 91 degrees West Longitude and between 30 and 35 degrees North Latitude. Approximately 2,900,000 people live in Mississippi. Mississippi covers approximately 48,000 square miles, making it the 35th largest state in the United States. To the north of Mississippi is Tennessee, the Volunteer State, with a population of 5,800,000. Arkansas, the Natural State and Louisiana, the Pelican State, border Mississippi to the west. They have a population of 2,700,000 and 4,500,000, respectively. Alabama, with a population of 4,500,000, forms the eastern border.

four
4

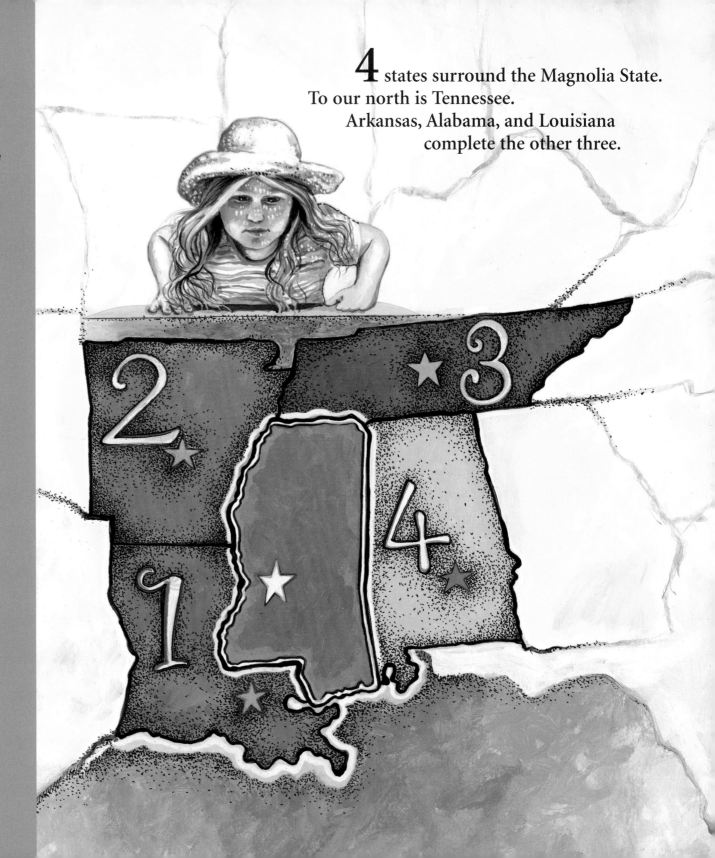

4 states surround the Magnolia State.
To our north is Tennessee.
Arkansas, Alabama, and Louisiana
complete the other three.

5 famous writers from Mississippi
put our state on the map.
Is there anything better in the whole wide world
than a good book in your lap?

Margarett Walker Alexander

Tennessee Williams

Eudora Welty

Willie Morris

William Faulkner

Some of America's greatest writers were born or lived much of their lives in Mississippi. Their works often reflected life in the Magnolia State.

A Nobel Prize winner, William Faulkner (1897-1962) moved to Oxford as a young child. He set many of his novels and short stories in Yoknapatawpha County.

Tennessee Williams (1911-1983) was born in Columbus and is considered one of America's best playwrights. *The Glass Menagerie* contains autobiographical elements from his Mississippi life.

A Pulitzer Prize winner, Eudora Welty (1909-2001) was a lifelong resident of Jackson. Her fairy tale, *The Robber Bridegroom*, was set along the Natchez Trace.

Willie Morris (1934-1999) was born in Jackson, a sixth generation Mississippian. Many of his writings centered on life in the Delta.

Margaret Walker Alexander (1915-1998) first moved to Mississippi in 1949. Her works, mostly poetry, chronicled the life of southern African-American women.

five
5

Machines are built to help us work.
They make our jobs go quicker.
6 Mississippi cotton is sometimes picked by a row cotton picker.

Mississippi is one of the top three cotton producing states in America. The warm, moist weather and rich soil make growing cotton easy in Mississippi.

Cotton was once harvested by hand. It was hard, backbreaking work. Today, mechanical cotton pickers pull cotton from the stalk and blow it into a storage compartment. Once the container is full, the load is dumped into a wagon and taken to a cotton gin where the cotton seed is separated from the lint. The cotton is compressed into bales to save space. Each bale weighs approximately 500 pounds.

Cotton is used in a variety of ways including in the making of T-shirts, bath towels, bed linen, and dollar bills. Up to 75% of a dollar bill is made of cotton!

six

6

7 rough and tough young cowpokes
compete at the Dixie National Rodeo.
"Whoopee ti-yo, git along, little dogies,"
It's time to start the show.

Jackson, Mississippi hosts the Dixie National Rodeo every year in February. The rodeo is one of the largest rodeos east of the Mississippi. This event lasts three weeks and is jam-packed with events for visitors of all ages. Participants compete for awards in livestock shows with their horses, poultry, swine, cows, steers, lambs, and goats. In the Junior Roundup, Mississippi's 4-H and Future Farmers of America show their sheep, hogs, and cattle to win the "Grand Champion" award.

Aspiring beauty queens compete in the Miss Dixie National & Miss Rodeo Pageants. Bull riders, barrel racers, bulldoggers, and ropers compete for top prizes. Food, events, and clowns help make the Dixie National Rodeo an exciting event for thousands of cowpokes every year.

seven

7

African Americans who lived between the Mississippi and Yazoo Rivers at the time of the Civil War were some of the poorest people in America. Historians note the Mississippi Delta musical genre now called "The Blues" was born from chants, songs, and field hollers and usually involves sad feelings. Blues grew in popularity as musicians played in social clubs called juke joints.

During the first half of the twentieth century the boll weevil destroyed many cotton crops in the South. African Americans moved in large numbers from the agricultural South to large cities in the North in search of better paying jobs. Delta Blues musicians were among those traveling across America spreading their style of music.

Robert L. Johnson, a blues great, was born in Hazlehurst. Charlie Patton, born in Hinds County, has been called the King of Delta Blues. Today audiences all over the world enjoy Mississippi's original music: The Blues.

eight

8

8 talented blues musicians
keep the dance floor in full swing
by wailing songs from Charlie Patton,
Robert Johnson, and B.B. King.

9 largemouth bass might soon be caught
if they are not careful today.
This magnificent fish "was" a trophy catch,
but this time he got away!

There are approximately 175 species of freshwater fish in lakes, rivers, and ponds throughout Mississippi. The largemouth bass is one of the most sought-after fish in the state and was designated the official state fish in 1974.

Largemouth bass are black to green on the back with lighter sides and a pale stomach. A black line runs along the side of the body. An adult can grow to 21 inches in length and weigh up to 10 pounds.

Largemouth bass prefer to nest in clear, quiet, and vegetated water. The male builds a 2-3 foot nest by sweeping away debris with his head and tail. The female lays between 2,000 and 40,000 eggs and the male guards them until they hatch five to ten days later.

The state's largest largemouth bass was caught in the Natchez State Park Lake on December 31, 1992. It weighed a whopping 18.15 pounds.

nine
9

Mississippi has one of the largest play-grounds in the world! The world's longest artificially created beach stretches for 26 miles along Mississippi's Gulf coast. The average yearly temperature here is nearly 70 degrees. Because Mississippi's Gulf Coast has a temperate climate, visitors can enjoy this beach year-round. Visitors to this area sail, jet ski, parasail, or just sit near the water under beach umbrellas enjoying great books. Towns along this stretch of beach include Ocean Springs, Biloxi, Gulfport, Long Beach, Pass Christian, Bay St. Louis, and Waveland.

ten
10

10 colorful umbrellas are planted
along a sandy beach of white.
Kite flying, fishing, and castle building
make us all squeal with delight.

11 letters spell our state's name.
It's easy, give it a try:
Begin the fun with a capital M.
Keep going until the last letter I.

Mississippi is named for the mighty river that forms the state's western boundary. The name has Ojibwa (Native American) origins. *Missi* means big and *siippii* means river. Together, they form Mississippi or mighty river.

For some, spelling Mississippi is difficult. For others, there are funny rhymes or phrases to help them get it correct. Many people grow up spelling Mississippi by saying:

"M – I – crooked letter – crooked letter – I crooked letter – crooked letter – I humpback – humpback – I."

Two other ways to remember how to spell the state's name are:

"Mrs. M, Mrs. I, Mrs. Double S I, Mrs. Double S I, Mrs. Double P I."

"Four simple words will get you by: What you'll never MISS IS SIP PI."

eleven

11

12 bottles, icy cold are filled
with Barqs™ Root Beer.
Set a dozen out on a summer's day
and watch them disappear!

Edward Barq was born in New Orleans in 1871. He moved to France while very young. There he studied chemistry including how to mix flavors. At 19, Barq returned to New Orleans and opened a bottling company. In 1897 he and his new wife moved to Biloxi, Mississippi and bottled artesian water with soda flavors. Barq invented Barqs™ Root Beer in 1898 while living in Biloxi. The building in which this drink was first bottled still stands at 224 Keller Avenue. Root beer is a soft drink made from many ingredients including vanilla, molasses, cherry tree bark, licorice root, sarsaparilla root, sassafras root bark, nutmeg, and anise.

Today Mississippi's innovative soft drink is sold throughout the United States and is bottled by the Coca-Cola™ corporation.

twelve
12

The earliest known human habitation of the region now called Mississippi dates back 12,000 years. At that time, Indians hunted mastodon, saber-toothed tigers, and bison with crude spears.

Large villages developed in Mississippi approximately 2,000 years ago. Indians hunted with bows and arrows and used pottery for cooking and storage. The three sisters: corn, beans, and squash became staples for many meals.

In 1540 the first Europeans explored the Mississippi region. Spanish explorers brought foreign diseases with them. As a result, the Mississippi Indian population declined from 200,000 to just 20,000.

During the 1600s other European explorers navigated the Mississippi River and French explorers claimed this region. During the eighteenth century, English and Spanish forces also fought for the land.

On December 10, 1817, Congress admitted Mississippi as the 20th state to the Union.

twenty

20

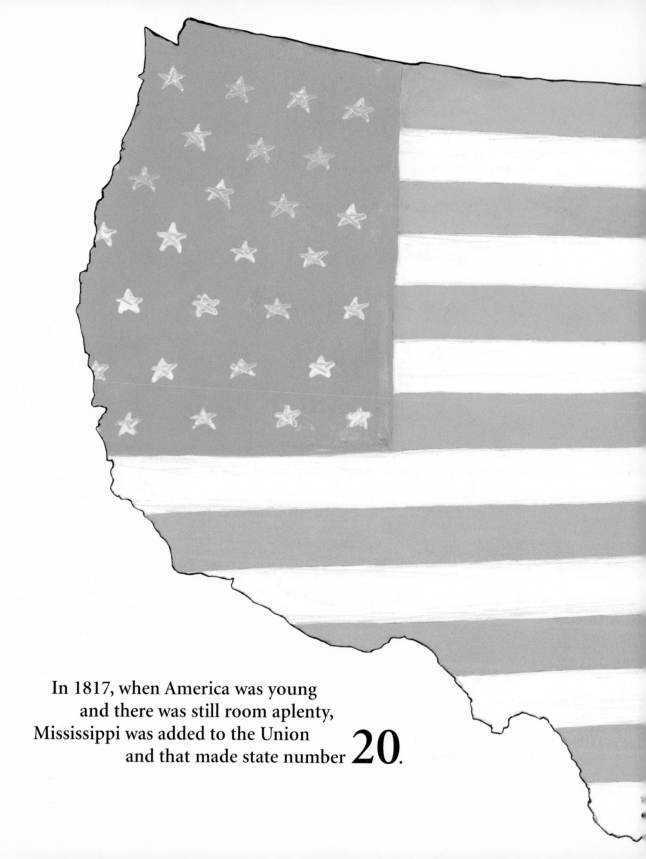

In 1817, when America was young
and there was still room aplenty,
Mississippi was added to the Union
and that made state number 20.

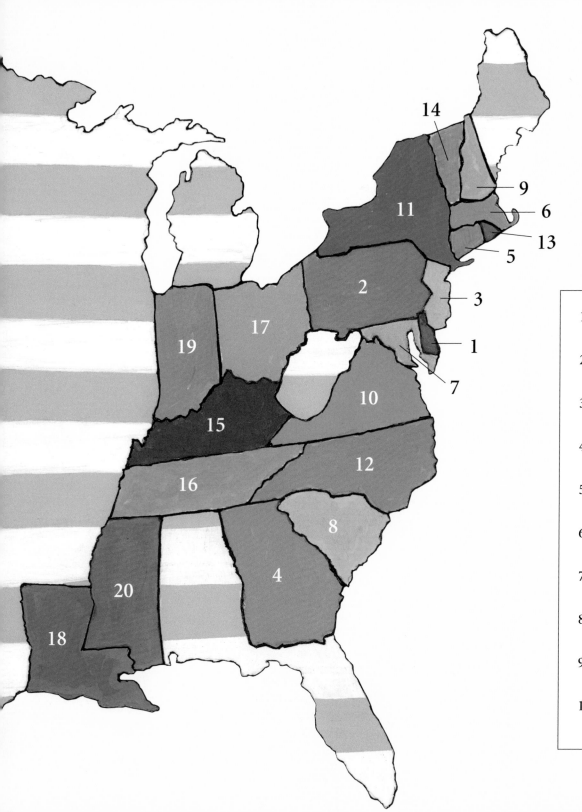

1. Delaware
   December 7, 1787

2. Pennsylvania
   December 12, 1787

3. New Jersey
   December 18, 1787

4. Georgia
   January 2, 1788

5. Connecticut
   January 9, 1788

6. Massachusetts
   February 6, 1788

7. Maryland
   April 28, 1788

8. South Carolina
   May 23, 1788

9. New Hampshire
   June 21, 1788

10. Virginia
    June 25, 1788

11. New York
    July 26, 1788

12. North Carolina
    November 21, 1789

13. Rhode Island
    May 29, 1790

14. Vermont
    March 4, 1791

15. Kentucky
    June 1, 1792

16. Tennessee
    June 1, 1796

17. Ohio
    March 1, 1803

18. Louisiana
    April 30, 1812

19. Indiana
    December 11, 1816

20. Mississippi
    December 10, 1817

Called the "Mad Potter of Biloxi" young artist George E. Ohr dug Mississippi clay from the banks of the Tchoutacabouffa River and transformed it into beautiful mugs, saucers, cups, and pots. Born in Mississippi in 1857, Ohr was an extraordinary talent, and earned the title "America's First Art Potter."

Many types of clay cover most of Mississippi. Potters use Mississippi ball clay and their hands to form lovely pieces of art. This pottery, called greenware, is placed in a kiln and baked at temperatures of over 2,000 degrees Fahrenheit to make it rock hard. Sometimes, if the clay has air pockets or impurities, it explodes in the kiln and is useless. If the clay "survives the fire" it is now called earthenware or stoneware, depending on the temperature of the kiln. Earthenware is a final product, but after stoneware cools, artists color or glaze it and put it back into the kiln for a second firing. The end result is a beautiful piece of pottery made of Mississippi clay and by Mississippi hands!

thirty
30

30 pieces of pottery
make lovely pieces of art.
Although carefully sculpted by loving hands,
their beauty pours straight from the heart.

40 pear shaped oyster shells
are headed for a plate.
Harvested just off our shore,
they're the official shell of our state.

The oyster shell was selected as the official state shell of the Magnolia State on April 12, 1974.

Oystering began in Mississippi over 10,000 years ago. Native Americans used the oyster shells for tools, jewelry, and money. Two hundred years ago Biloxi was known as the "Oyster Capital of the World" as oysters were shipped from Mississippi to many parts of the United States.

Oysters are born as microscopic organisms in temperate waters. That means the water is warm all year. They thrive where salt and fresh water mix together. If growing in uncrowded locations, oysters live to a ripe old age of 20. The pear shaped oyster grows to 10 centimeters in length.

Many of Mississippi's oysters are harvested from the western Mississippi Sound. From a boat, oystermen scoop oysters from the bottom of the Sound by dredging or with huge tongs that look like two garden rakes.

forty
40

Children: be sure to get permission and help from an adult before starting this tasty treat.

Mississippi Mud Cake
Ingredients:
1 cup butter
½ cup cocoa
2 cups sugar
4 eggs, beaten
1½ cups flour
pinch of salt
1½ cups nuts, chopped
1 tsp vanilla
marshmallows — to garnish

Directions:
- Melt butter and cocoa together
- Stir in sugar and beaten eggs
- Mix well
- Add flour, salt, chopped nuts, and vanilla; mix well
- Spoon batter into a greased 13x9x2 inch pan and bake at 350 degrees for 35 to 45 minutes
- Sprinkle marshmallows on top of warm cake; cover with your favorite chocolate frosting

fifty
50

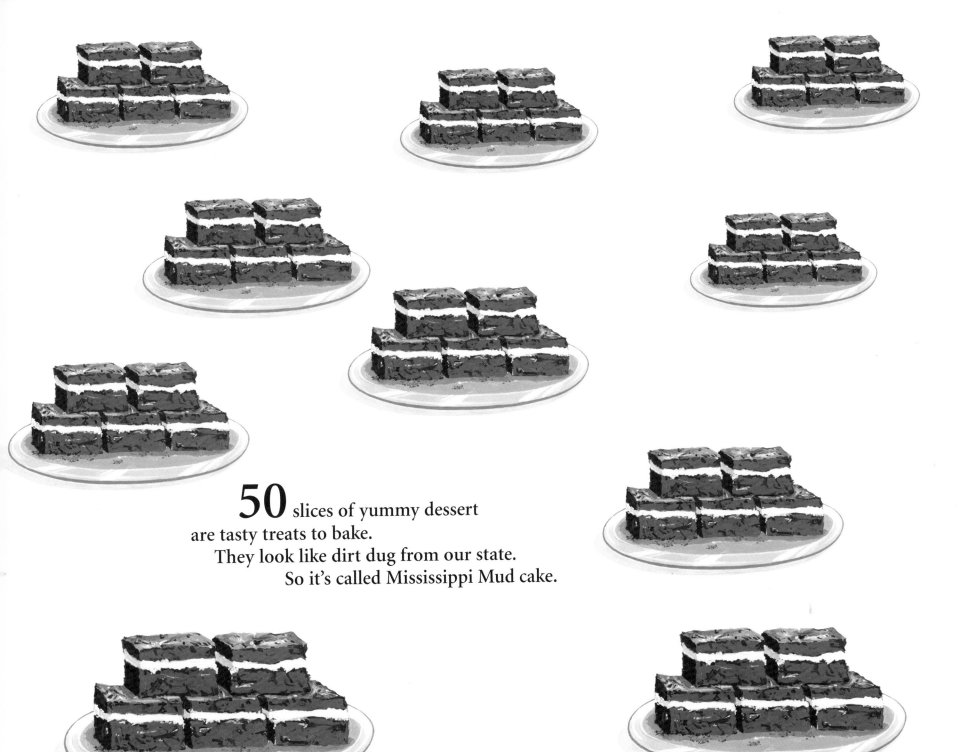

50 slices of yummy dessert
are tasty treats to bake.
They look like dirt dug from our state.
So it's called Mississippi Mud cake.

60 pecans are ready to crack
and put in pies with caramel,
or maybe in pralines, cookies, fudge,
or eaten straight from their shell.

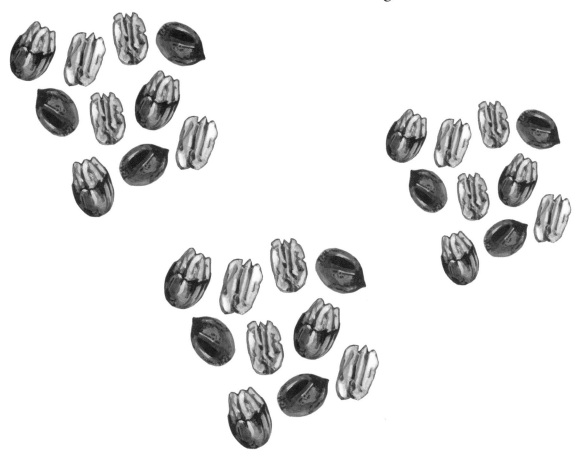

Agriculture is the number one industry in Mississippi and pecans play an important part. Mississippi has between 14,000 and 16,000 acres of pecan orchards. The Magnolia State is one of the top 10 producers of pecans in America with Mississippi pecan growers producing approximately 7 million pounds of pecans each year. Bolivar, Coahoma, and Tallahatchie counties are major producers of pecans.

This important nut provides over 19 vitamins and minerals, including a much-needed source of protein, iron, calcium, potassium, phosphorus, several B vitamins, and zinc.

Pecans last up to nine months in a refrigerator and over two years if stored in a freezer. Besides their great taste, pecans are rich in antioxidants, substances that help fight diseases like Alzheimer's, Parkinson's, cancer, and heart disease.

National Pecan Month is celebrated in April.

sixty
60

Shrimp are an important industry along Mississippi's gulf coast. The wetlands there provide the ideal place for shrimp to spawn and grow. A female shrimp releases between 100,000 to 1,000,000 eggs. It takes only 24 hours for shrimp to hatch.

The Mississippi shrimp season traditionally begins the first or second week in June. Three types of shrimp are commercially harvested: white, pink, and brown. The brown shrimp make up 85% of all shrimp collected in Mississippi's waters. If not eaten by fish or caught by anglers, shrimp may live to be two years old.

Although the boat featured on this page is called a "double-rigged shrimp trawler," it doesn't take a boat to harvest shrimp. Individuals can fling a "cast net" from docks to snag their dinner. Millions of pounds of shrimp are netted each year in the waters of the Magnolia State.

seventy

70

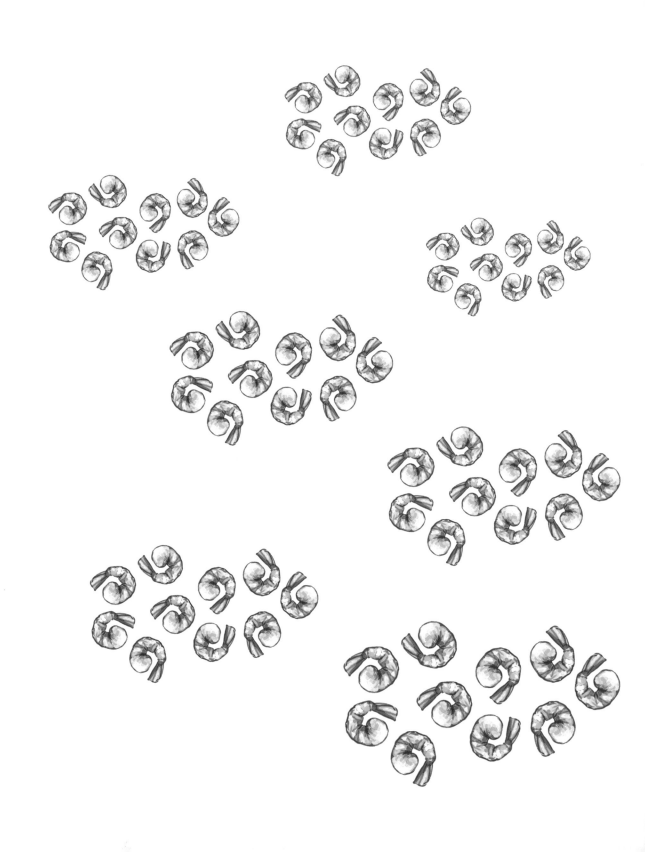

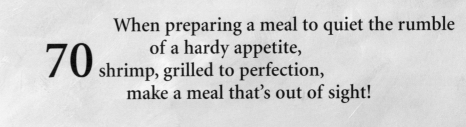

70 When preparing a meal to quiet the rumble
of a hardy appetite,
shrimp, grilled to perfection,
make a meal that's out of sight!

80 checkers are way too many.
     Stack the extras in rows of ten.
I have to warn you before we start:
     I always play to win!

Petal, Mississippi is home to the American Checker Federation and International Checker Hall of Fame. Nobody knows for sure how old the game of checkers is, but ancient hieroglyphics, including drawings on King Tut's pyramid in Egypt, depicted players playing a game on a checkerboard. Archeologists predict the game is at least 5,000 years old.

Checkers is played on a board with 64 squares, arranged on an 8"x8" grid. Each player moves 12 "men" or checkers diagonally forward onto vacant squares. Jumping over an opponent's piece to an adjacent vacant square captures that piece.

Once a checker reaches the opposite end of the board, called the crownhead, it becomes a king. A king can move in any direction as long as it does not jump its own checkers.

The object of checkers is to capture all of the opponent's pieces or block them so they cannot move or jump when it is their turn to move.

eighty
80

As with 14 other states, the honeybee is the official insect of Mississippi! In the wild, honeybees create intricate nests called hives. Hives contain up to 20,000 bees during the summer months. Domestic hives may have up to 80,000 bees.

Honeybees are either: queens, drones, or workers. Each hive has only one queen. She lays over 1,500 eggs per day and lives two to eight years.

Drones are males and live about eight weeks. Their only job is to mate with the queen. Each hive contains several hundred drones.

Worker bees are females and maintain the hive by constructing it, tending the queen and drones, cleaning, defending the hive, and gathering nectar. Workers live between 6 weeks to 6 months, depending on the time of year they are born.

Honeybees visit up to 50 flowers in an hour. It takes approximately 30,000 trips to flowers for bees to make one pound of honey. Mississippi honeybees produce over 1,400,000 pounds of honey a year.

ninety
90

90 hardworking honeybees
fly from flower to flower to flower.
They carry nectar back to their hive
hour after hour after hour.

100 Coreopsis blooms
grow yellow like the sun.
They sprout wild across the countryside.
Can you count them one-by-one?

The *Coreopsis lanceolata*, also known as tickseed, is Mississippi's official state wildflower. Coreopsis flowers are easy to care for as they grow best in rocky or sandy soil, along roadsides or in old fields. They are a favorite food for goldfinches. The flower is approximately 2 inches wide and blooms in clumps on 2-3 foot stalks. Coreopsis blooms from May to June.

one
hundred
100

Michael Shoulders

Michael Shoulders, Ed. D., has been an educator for more than 28 years. He received his doctorate from Tennessee State University. Michael enjoys conducting author visits at schools and speaking about literacy issues to students, teachers, and parents. This is Michael's fifth book with Sleeping Bear Press. His titles include *M is for Magnolia: A Mississippi Alphabet* and *V is for Volunteer: A Tennessee Alphabet*. Michael is a proud member of the International Reading Association.

Michael lives in Clarksville, Tennessee with his wife Debbie. They have three children, Jason, Ryan, and Meghann. Learn more about Michael at www.michaelshoulders.com.

Rick Anderson

Rick grew up in the Mississippi Delta, earned a master's degree in Art Education from Delta State University, and began his teaching career in 1975 in Greenville, Mississippi. He retired from the classroom in 1993 to continue his artistic career. As a professional artist, Rick has exhibited throughout the United States and has won numerous awards.

1 Mississippi, 2 Mississippi: A Mississippi Number Book, is Rick's fourth book with Sleeping Bear Press. He also illustrated *M is for Magnolia: A Mississippi Alphabet*. Rick is also an International Reading Association member.

He lives in Clinton, Mississippi, with his wife Merrie. They have one son, Denman. Learn more about Rick at www.rickandersonart.com.